FIRST STEPS
to Thriving in Recovery™

Disclaimer:
The author, Garret Biss, is not is not a licensed medical or mental health professional. Nothing offered by Garret Biss is intended to treat, diagnose, or cure any mental health or medical condition. The contents of workbook is for informational and/or educational purposes only and is not intended to be a substitute for professional medical advice, diagnosis, or treatment.

This publication contains the opinions and ideas of its author. It is intended to provide helpful and informative material on the subjects addressed within. It is provided with the understanding that the author is not engaged in rendering medical, health, or any other kind of personal professional services in the workbook. The author specifically disclaims all responsibility for any liability, loss, or risk, personal or otherwise, which is incurred as a consequence, directly or indirectly, of the use and application of any of the contents of this workbook. Use of the information in this workbook is to be used at your own discretion and your own risk.

Cover Photo by Jonathon Reed on Unsplash
Cover and Layout Designed by Christine Farver, *New Bern Magazine*

Dear friend,

This workbook is designed to help bring joy and fulfillment into your life while living in recovery. You might be using this book as part of a workshop or as a self-study guide in the comfort of your home. However you use it, this workbook will guide you through your FIRST STEPS to Thriving in Recovery and experiencing living a life unchained from the consequences of your past.

I've discovered that too many people in recovery find themselves held back by the emotional and personal consequences of their time in active addiction or substance use disorder. These effects perpetuate the negative self-talk, guilt, shame, and lack of self-esteem that keeps people from living into their joy and experiencing the life that they want and deserve.

As part of my own recovery, I've spent the last 10 years studying human potential and the science of human flourishing. I set out to learn ways that people can not only experience a more successful recovery, but live into their higher potential.

I want better for you. As a human potential trainer and recovery mindset coach, I don't want you to merely survive your life in recovery; I want you to thrive! If you're not living into your dreams and you're not experiencing the happiness and the joy and the success that you desire, this workbook is for you. It will empower you to take the FIRST STEPS to Thriving in YOUR Recovery.

So turn the page, and let's get started.

Garret Biss
Creator of Thriving in YOUR Recovery™

STEP ONE

Give Credit Where Credit is Due

Step one is about taking some time to focus on what's good about you.

While living in recovery, we're too often reminded of the mistakes we've made in the past. In fact, you're probably more aware than the average person of your personal "defects" and the things that you've done wrong. If you spend a lot of time focusing on those defects, trying to correct them and make up for your wrongs, you're not alone. Many of us living in recovery do this.

But you can't build a better future by focusing on your failures. You can't build a foundation for living into your potential and experiencing joy and happiness if you're only focusing on what you've done wrong in the past. Instead, if we focus on our strengths and successes, we can begin laying a foundation for becoming a better version of ourselves.

It's time for you to take control by reminding yourself of your positive traits as well as the wins and successes you have had already. When you do, you lay a foundation on which to build your future. You can't rely on the outside world to provide you with this insight or positive reminders – it has to come from within.

Part 1: I am excellent

On the lines below, list ten things you've excelled at in the past. These can be small things or big things. All that matters is you're great at them. (Set your modesty aside for a bit. Go ahead, no one's watching!!)

(Examples: I am great at math, I am great at crossword puzzles, I am great at driving)

1. _____
2. _____
3. _____
4. _____
5. _____
6. _____
7. _____
8. _____
9. _____
10. _____

When you start focusing on the good things and remind yourself of the good things that are within you, it helps you build a foundation to build your future on. It's healthy to be able to identify and remind ourselves of our strengths and positive qualities. Doing so is a good thing; it doesn't mean you are arrogant or cocky.

Part 2: I am successful

Now I want you to list twenty-one wins or successes you've had in your life. You can start small with things like learning to walk or graduating fifth grade. Don't forget the fact that you've found yourself in recovery! Give yourself credit for the tremendous courage and willpower that started you on this path. If you are having trouble, try breaking your life into three parts, Birth until [1/3 your age], [2/3 your age], until now. Then list seven for each part.

(examples: Had a child, started a career, improved my golf score, learned to walk, graduated 3rd grade, learned to read, got a job, etc. Don't question whether anything was too big or too small for the list; just write it!)

1. _____

2. _____

3. _____

4. _____

5. _____

6. _____

7. _____

8. _____

9. _____

10. _____

11. _____

12. _____

13. _____

14. _____

15. _____

16. _____

17. _____

18. _____

19. _____

20. _____

21. _____

Part 3: I am positive

Think about three positive qualities or characteristics that define you. They might be qualities your boss would use to describe you (if your boss likes and appreciates you) or the reasons why your friends enjoy your company. Think about the things that really exemplify who you are as an individual.

Although you could just write single words here, this exercise is more powerful if you write it like this: "I am compassionate. I am detail-oriented. I am..." By stating it this way, you're really taking ownership of your positive qualities.

(examples: I am ambitious. I am driven. I am creative. I am a good listener. I am a great writer.)

1. _____

2. _____

3. _____

Part 4: Recap and Reflection

Our past addictive behaviors have many consequences that we must overcome. Often the last to improve is our self-esteem and confidence in our own true ability and talents. Years of feeling out of control, of people pointing out our faults, of hiding our true feelings and pain from others behind the masks we wear all cause us to lose touch with our authentic selves and our natural, innate wisdom and power.

We can't count on others to give these things back to us once we are focused on our recovery. It's up to us. The three exercises above are a few of the most effective tools to experience an immediate change in the way we feel about ourselves. By taking some time to reflect on this experience – how it felt, what you learned, what you enjoyed about it – you can anchor this positive change and make a greater impact to your self-esteem and personal strength.

At the end of these three exercises, take a little time to reflect. How did you feel? Was it difficult? Did you feel uneasy? For many people, this is a hard exercise to complete. You may have taken the easy way out and just written down a bunch of little things or failed to complete all the lists. That's ok. If you gave the exercises an honest effort and put something down then you have started a process of seeing and recognizing the strengths and abilities you have within.

You can journal about the experience of this First Step in the space below.

_____

_____

_____

_____

_____

_____

This exercise often reminds me of the famous quote by Dr. Martin Luther King, "Darkness cannot drive out darkness; only light can do that. Hate cannot drive out hate; only love can do that."

We cannot drive out the darkness and the demons that reside in us by focusing on that darkness; by focusing on the good that lives in every one of us, we can overcome that darkness and become the person we want to be. By focusing on the bad things we've done or the defects we possess, we merely fuel our tendency toward emotions of guilt, shame, and self-hate. Focusing on the things we love and respect about ourselves fuels greater emotions of confidence, love, and respect.

If these exercises in Step One made you more than a little uncomfortable, I highly encourage you to revisit this part of your workbook often. Take the time to remind yourself regularly of the good in yourself and the good things you've done. Focus on these positive qualities so you can build that stronger foundation. Thriving in your recovery starts with being able to see the good in yourself.

Next, think about the places where you haven't given yourself proper credit for your positive qualities. In what areas of your life do you do this?

_____

_____

_____

_____

_____

If your mindset is based on those areas where you're falling down, it deflates your self-esteem. So, reflect on the good emotions that came up during these exercises. If there's a certain area of your life where you feel like you're excelling, focus on that. **In the space below, write about the positive emotions that came up while making your lists. Excitement, joy, renewed passion?**

_____

_____

_____

_____

_____

Finally, how can you remember to give credit where credit is due and focus on your strengths? Do you have a supportive friend that can help you reflect every few weeks? Can you set a time at the end of the day or the week to reflect on the things you did well? **Make a commitment to do so and write it below. "I commit to….":**

_____

_____

STEP TWO

Joys, Purpose, and Passion

When we're living in active addiction, we tend to forget about those things that brought us natural joy and happiness. These activities tend to disappear from our lives as we focus more on a substance or behavior or on the pain that led us toward addiction in the first place.

There are many things in life that can bring natural sources of joy and excitement, but when we misuse something or are addicted to something for too long, our ability to naturally create those good feelings begins to diminish. Our addictions become a stand-in for the things we once enjoyed. Since we cannot selectively numb our emotions, when we use a substance or behavior as a way to escape, avoid, or numb a discomfort within us, we also numb the feelings of happiness, excitement, and joy that healthy activities once provided. An addiction actually blocks these good feelings because of the effects it has on our brain and because of the new habits that we've created.

In recovery, it's important to bring those natural sources of joy, enjoyment, and passion back into your life. If you're new in recovery or you spent a long time in substance use disorder or active addiction, you might have forgotten the many things that brought you joy and purpose.

When you start bringing those healthy sources of joy back into your life, they empower you to live into and thrive in your recovery.

Part 1: What brings me joy?

The activities we do when we feel "in the zone" or "swept away", are things that cause the release of many of the endorphins and feel good hormones that our bodies naturally create. When we exercise, experience new things, escape our worries and focus our time on being with friends, all of these things help stimulate those natural neuropathways that lead to sensations of euphoria, joy, and excitement. We often forget what these things are for us and many times we can forget to engage in these activities.

The last time I did this exercise, it reminded me how much I used to enjoy going for a walk in the woods, mountain biking, going skiing, and taking some time to read (without an agenda). These are simple things that I can do (some for little or no money) which help me release the stress that builds up in my life, and help me stimulate those natural pathways for positive feelings and emotions.

Make a list of things that bring joy and excitement. What are activities that you do that bring joy? This is an area you may need to revisit often. Sometimes we can get too focused on work or what we have to do, and we forget to take time for ourselves. This happens to everyone. Making a list can help you refocus on those things that really bring you joy.

It's okay if some of these cost money. You can budget for them. But make sure there are a few things on the list that are free or low cost. Also, try to think of things you can do alone and things you can do with friends or family.

(examples: mountain bike riding, taking a walk, quietly reading a book, going to the movies, playing with your kids)

1. _____

2. _____

3. _____

4. _____

5. _____

6. _____

7. _____

8. _____

9. _____

10. _____

11. _____

12. _____

13. _____

14. _____

15. _____

16. _____

17. _____

18. _____

19. _____

20. _____

Make time for these things or bring them top-of-mind so you can do them spontaneously when you have time. Start planning for those that require a little organization or some money. This is your happiness and your recovery...it's worth the time, effort, and expense.

Make sure your list of activities is a good balance of things you can do with friends and things you can do alone, things that cost money and things that don't, things that need to be planned and things you can do spontaneously. If there is something that you used to love to do but haven't done it in the past 5 years (or since your addiction got out of control), put a star next to it and try to do that sometime soon.

With all of these activities, use your own judgment. Don't put yourself in situations where you will likely be overcome by triggers. Don't engage in something if you know there will be too much temptation or too many people that will try to pressure you into something you don't want to do.

One obstacle many of us face when we think of doing something for ourselves is we are reminded of all the responsibilities we have, the things we haven't completed, or we think of many reasons we "don't deserve" to do something for ourselves. I am just as guilty of thinking, "I didn't get nearly enough done at work today and have many things to take care of at home. There is no way I can go 'play' right now or sit back and enjoy something good."

In reality, the more we neglect doing things just for us, things we personally enjoy, the more everything else suffers. The less productive we become, the grumpier we become, the less we diffuse the pain and stress within us, AND the more we jeopardize our recovery. That's a risk we should not take and a cost we cannot afford to pay.

I implore you to take this step seriously. Don't just put it on paper, make a plan to bring these things into your life.

Foster Connection

Many addiction and recovery experts now agree that the opposite of addiction isn't sobriety, it's connection. Remember to include things that you can do with other people, things that help foster that connection and healthy relationships.

Finding things that you can do with others—things that don't include or trigger your former addiction—is vital for your recovery; we all need connection. That doesn't just mean time at work, in 12-step meeting rooms, or home with the family. Travel somewhere, go to the park or the beach. Play a community sport or find a workout partner. Join a club that engages with a hobby you enjoy. Take a class at a community center and make some new friends.

Break It Down:

One technique is to break your list out into different categories. Some might overlap, for example, I can go mountain biking alone or with friends. In that case, put it on both lists.

Things I can do alone

_____

_____

_____

Things I can do with friends

_____

_____

_____

Things that cost money

_____

_____

_____

Things that are free

_____

_____

_____

Make a copy of this list and leave it somewhere you'll see it regularly (on your phone, on the fridge or on your bathroom mirror). Next time you're feeling down or need some extra joy, you'll have ideas of what to do.

This list can also be useful when you're fighting a craving and need to refocus your attention. Sometimes when cravings come up it's hard to remember what we need to do. Our go-to is to call a sponsor or get to a meeting, but it's important that we can also help ourselves by doing things that are specific to us and our joys.

Part 2: What is my purpose?

The greatest sense of fulfillment comes when we find and engage in something that is our unique purpose. A sense of meaning and purpose is important to anyone; this sense is necessary for a fulfilling life. For those of us in recovery, this is a critical element for maintaining recovery. The upward pull of purpose and a meaning-filled life is sometimes the only thing that helps us fight that downward pull of cravings and old behaviors.

Finding your purpose takes work, but it's well worth the effort. Many find that the joys they have in life helped them identify where their purpose lies.

I've found that my purpose is to share a message that inspires and empowers other people toward a happier and more fulfilling life. I want to help people break free from the chains of their addiction and their past so they can live into their potential and experience a better tomorrow.

I came to that conclusion because the different things that bring the most joy into my life are elements that support that mission. When my passions in life began to align more directly to the work I was doing, I found myself living in alignment with my purpose.

Disclaimer: Everyone's purpose is unique to them. For some people, their job doesn't fulfill their purpose. Sometimes work is just a way to pay the bills so you have the money and leisure to do something that does fulfill your purpose. That's perfectly fine.

Finding your purpose is something you can go to week-long workshops for or spend years working to discover. The following is just a quick exercise that can help you get some direction and figure out where to start. Before you start the exercise below, I recommend you read the section about understanding different types of happiness. This will bring some clarity as to why meaning and purpose is such an important part of life and a vital part of recovery.

Understanding different types of happiness

There are two kinds of happiness. The one you're probably more familiar with is hedonic happiness. This is happiness caused by an action or experience. It's the happiness we get from riding a roller coaster or watching our favorite TV show. It is also the sensation of happiness we experience when we indulge in something we like or expose ourselves to substances and behaviors that provide momentary euphoria. Hedonic happiness is caused by the things that come into our life but as soon as the thing is gone or the experience is over, the happiness fades.

The other form is eudaimonic (you-de-mon-ic) happiness. This is the happiness you get from finding your purpose and meaning in life. It is much more enduring than hedonic happiness and creates a greater, longer-lasting positive emotion. Most importantly, it doesn't break down as easily because of stress; it actually enables us to overcome stress and live into that best version of ourselves.

Hedonic happiness – a fleeting emotion; tied to experience or external object.

Eudaimonic happiness – enduring happiness; derived from engaging in one's purpose and from living a life of meaning.

Finding your purpose

List two of your unique positive qualities. You can look back to step three of part one or just write down whatever comes to mind right now.

(example: compassionate, caring, creative)

1. _____

2. _____

Next, list two ways that you enjoy expressing those qualities. When do they show up for you the most? How do you like to use them? How do you share them with the world?

(examples: supporting others, solving puzzles, creating a form of art, making beautiful things)

1. _____

2. _____

Part 3: How can I put my positive qualities to work pursuing my purpose?

Imagine a perfect world. In this world, there are unlimited resources and everyone is happy. What would that ideal world look like? How would you know it if you saw it? Write a paragraph explaining how you would interact with other people. Describe how you would spend your time.

Write this in the present tense, as though it's happening right now. What do you see, feel, and experience?

_____

_____

_____

_____

_____

_____

_____

_____

Bonus: My purpose is

You can get the most from this part by taking everything we've done so far and putting it together. Write a paragraph that explains what your life purpose is.

(example: My purpose is to use my compassion and ability to articulate a message that supports and empowers others so everyone is having fun, living into their potential and making a contribution that helps make the world a better place for all.)

There's no pressure to find your life's purpose right now, today. You can try something for a little while and see how it feels. If it doesn't seem to fit, or you don't stay excited about it, you can always try something new. You don't have to pick a purpose and commit to it for the rest of your life; you're just looking for a purpose to "date" right now.

Come back to this part anytime you feel like you need a stronger sense of direction.

If you have some experience meditating and would like to try a guided visualization to help find your purpose, see the resource section at the back of this workbook.

STEP THREE

Goals and Desires

By now you should feel more aware of yourself and more empowered. You've taken two small steps. Now you're taking a slightly bigger step by looking at your goals and desires.

Part 1: What I want

Make a list of things you want to do, be or have. Where do you want to invest your positive qualities and emotions? If everything was possible, what would you do? What are your dreams? Your ambitions? Don't let the past restrict you.

Write down 10-15 things you'd like to be, do, or have in your life.

(examples: travel to Spain, visit Niagara Falls, buy a boat, get married)

1. _____

2. _____

3. _____

4. _____

5. _____

6. _____

7. _____

8. _____

9. _____

10. _____

11. _____

12. _____

13. _____

14. _____

15. _____

You can make a much longer list if you want to. If this exercise really inspires you, I challenge you to write down 100 things. There are no limits here, but for the purposes of part one, write down at least 10-15.

Having goals helps you focus your attention. It helps you invest your time and resources wisely. We've all spent time in our lives investing in things we didn't even really want; maybe we could have spent that time and energy focused on things that would make us feel happy and fulfilled.

Remember, hedonic happiness is tied to an external experience or object, while, eudaimonic happiness comes from living a life of meaning.

You get a spike of hedonic happiness when you achieve a goal, but that happiness fades as soon as you get used to your new reality. On the other hand, when you make progress toward your goals, that progress gives you a sense of eudaimonic happiness. You're happy because you're working toward something that you feel is worth having or that fulfills your life purpose.

Some benefits of eudaimonic happiness: lasts a lot longer, builds up your self-esteem and shows you that you can believe in yourself. If you don't have any goals that you are working toward, you miss out on the opportunity to feel eudaimonic happiness by working toward something meaningful.

Part 2: What I want to achieve

Now you're going to identify some things you'd like to achieve. One way to do this is to look at areas of your life where you are most out of balance. In step one, we focused on the areas we were succeeding in. Once we have that joy and clarity, it's okay to focus on those things that are lacking so we can clean up these areas and start achieving our goals.

For example, you might be doing well professionally, but your personal health is struggling. Or you might be in great shape, but your finances are a mess. It's essential to clean up these areas so you're not limited by these things. No matter how successful you are in some areas, if you're really deficient in another area it can steal the joy from your successes. Any area where your success and fulfillment are lacking is an area that challenges your recovery.

Start with a quick self-assessment. While considering the list of areas of life below, pick a number between 1 and 10 and rate where you stand in that area of your life.

(example: Zero means you're entirely off-track, 10 means you've achieved the ideal)

The Flourishing Center® recognizes six areas of life that are pathways to flourishing:

1. **Positivity:** A propensity toward positive emotions, an optimistic outlook, emotional resilience, and positive self-talk.

2. **Engagement:** Involvement in activities or projects that are positive and fulfilling, challenging and rewarding.

3. **Relationships:** Having sufficient authentic connections at work, home, and in the community that provide nurturing and support.

4. **Meaning and Purpose:** A motivation that drives a person toward a satisfying future; a clear sense of what is important and most fulfilling in one's life.

5. **Achievement:** Regular, measurable progress toward meaningful goals in one's personal and/or professional life.

6. **Vitality:** Physical and emotional health; energetic and vibrant, without dis-ease.

In a well-balanced life, the goal isn't to achieve perfect tens in every area. Instead, you're striving to continuously grow and improve. I would consider a life where every area is an 8 or above as a life where you are thriving and expressing your real potential.

Part 3: What I'm working on

Look at where your life is most out of balance so you can spend some energy on those areas. Identify those places that are lacking the most. Some areas might be more important to you than others right now, and that's fine. Choose one place that's lacking and feels important to you and focus on that in the next few steps.

Even if you have several areas that you'd like to improve, just pick one or two for now. Once you get those first areas where you'd like them to be, you can move on to another area that needs improvement. (My suggestion: If your personal health and vitality are lacking, I would recommend starting on this area first. When our energy is depleted and we just don't feel well, it can be difficult to effect any changes in our life. When we feel good, it makes everything else a little easier to manage and to change.)

The area that requires the most attention is:

_____

The different areas of your life all affect each other. If you're struggling in one, that struggle is probably influencing other areas of your life. Write about how your score in this area might be affecting the rest of your life.

(example: My poor health means I'm not performing as well as I could at work and I don't have much energy to engage with my family when I get home.)

_____

_____

_____

_____

_____

_____

_____

_____

Fortunately, because the different areas of your life are connected, when you improve one part, everything improves. Write about how improving that one area of your life will positively influence other areas.

(example: If I feel better and have more energy, I can contribute more at work and spend time engaging with my family in a positive and meaningful way.)

_____

_____

_____

_____

_____

_____

_____

_____

Now set three goals that you would like to achieve in that area to help you move in a positive direction. Try setting one short-term goal, one medium-term goal, and one long-term goal.

(example: I want to make a habit of going to the gym 3x/week. I want to run a 5K in less than 25 minutes. I want to fit into my old pants by next summer).

Goal 1: _____

Goal 2: _____

Goal 3: _____

Setting short, medium, and long-term goals helps you keep your attention focused on what's important to you. If you set only long-term goals, you might get distracted before you've made a real difference in your life.

If you still aren't buying into this need for goals in your life, consider the old saying:

"Life is about the journey, not the destination."

A similar sentiment applies to goals. Although the positive emotion of achieving your goal may be fleeting, you can derive happiness from perceived progress toward a goal. It's not always about whether you achieve it or not; progress alone is sometimes enough. When you can see that you are progressing toward a goal that is important to you, it stimulates a great feeling. If you have no clearly defined goals that you are working toward, this significant source of happiness is completely missing from your life.

One awesome thing is, it doesn't have to be some life-changing, earth-shattering goal to create this emotion. A simple goal like saving $500, straightening up the house, or purging some closets can work. As long as you can "perceive progress to achieving the goal," you are all set. Of course, setting a goal that will take longer – 3 months, 1 year – means you can enjoy that happiness ride even longer.

Part 4: I have resources

Just like in step one when you focused on your positive qualities and past wins, we're now going to look at those areas in your life where you have sevens and above. These high numbers show you that you have positive qualities or resources that you can use to invest in your future.

What can you learn from what you're doing in those areas? Maybe you can take some of those same practices or habits and apply them to other areas of your life. Or perhaps it's not something you do, but it's something about who you are as a person. These personal characteristics are strengths you can use in all areas of your life.

Remember, one area where you are succeeding is in your recovery. What is it that helped you get to recovery? What is it about you as an individual? Maybe it's a great support system or a loving friend. Maybe it's your willpower, your courage, your determination. How can you use some of those things to make a positive impact on some area where you may be struggling?

The areas of my life that are most fulfilling are:

_____

_____

These are the qualities and resources that have helped me be successful in those areas:

_____

_____

_____

_____

_____

_____

_____

_____

_____

_____

Conclusion: Next steps

Too often, when we look at the places where we fail, we focus on all the reasons that we're deficient in that area. All that does is disempower us and start us on a downward spiral. Let's not do that. Let's focus on your strengths. Congratulations on taking your first steps!

If you've done all of the exercises, you are already leaning into your higher potential. As you live out some of your joys, engage in things that bring you purpose, and perceive progress toward your goals, your happiness, joy, and fulfillment will grow.

As you grow in your recovery, you may want to return to these steps. Every time you do, you'll learn something new and gain a deeper understanding of yourself. These exercises will empower you to live into your potential, to thrive more in your recovery and make a positive impact in your life.

If you're ready to continue this journey, I'm here to support you. Helping you thrive in recovery is my purpose in life. If there's something that I can do to help you navigate your path to thriving in recovery, please reach out. I'd love to connect.

ABOUT GARRET BISS

I am a retired Marine Corps Pilot. Transitioning from a career of military service was a traumatic chapter of my life – one defined by near-constant anxiety, regular panic attacks, and a battle with substance use. Through surviving the experience, I began a journey of personal discovery and a search for purpose and meaning in life. This journey led me to earn a Certificate in Applied Positive Psychology (CAPP) from The Flourishing Center™ , and a certification as a human-potential trainer from the Canfield Training Group following a year-long mentorship with America's #1 Success Coach, Jack Canfield (co-creator of the Chicken Soup for the Soul series). I have used my education and my own experience to create the Thriving in YOUR Recovery™ program with a mission to serve others who are facing a similar struggle.

Through my professional experience, education, and personal life journey, I've cultivated a wealth of valuable insight and resources for overcoming adversity, developing resilience against addiction, and finding ways to use a troubled past and the challenges of today to build a better tomorrow.

I currently live in New Bern, North Carolina. When I'm not traveling around the world speaking or serving my favorite non-profit, One Million Goal (OneMillionGoal.org), I can be found loitering in a coffee shop, snapping pictures of a sunset, or strolling the town with "mini-me" (my daughter KK).

About me as a Recovery Mindset Coach

I understand my role as a recovery coach and advocate is to help others in recovery experience a better recovery journey and become better versions of themselves. It's not my role to define what one's recovery journey *should* look like or what success *should* mean to them.

Though the actions and behaviors or people who are struggling with addiction may look similar, each person's journey to that struggle with addiction was a unique path of experiences and circumstances – there are many pathways to addiction. Likewise, each person's journey to their best recovery is going to require a unique combination of tools, resources, and experiences – there are many pathways to recovery.

There is no one pathway to recovery that will serve everyone, nor serve them equally. And no single pathway to recovery is the perfect solution; each one has its advantages and drawbacks. I believe it is our job as people in recovery to find the best pathway for us. We do that by finding all that is available and learning what works best for us personally.

It's my role as a recovery mindset coach to help you learn what is available and help you craft the best plan for your recovery. I just want to help you get from where you are to where you want to be – whatever that looks like. And I will do that by helping you honestly assess where you are presently, clearly define where you want to go and make sure that your plan to get there addresses all areas of a well-developed life.

Please visit the resources below and connect with me if there is more I can do to serve you.
GarretBiss.com – Learn more about the work I do as a speaker, author, and coach
ThrivingInYourRecovery.com -- Find Resources, coaching, online courses
ALifeUnchained.com – Join a community of like-minded people on a similar journey
YouTube.com/GarretBBiss – Find inspiring videos, recorded presentations, and daily recovery wisdom

And find me on social media:

NEXT STEPS

The journey of a thousand miles begins with the first few steps. Sometimes, our lives can feel like a journey of a thousand miles, with seemingly no end to present challenges or struggles in sight. Now, you have taken those first steps to a better chapter of your life – a chapter of living into your higher potential for happiness, fulfillment, and success.

If you have lived a chapter of your life feeling unfulfilled, scared, alone, or uncertain about the future, your struggle does not have to continue. Recovery is a life-long journey and every successful journey requires you to continue moving. If you take the right steps, each one can bring you further from the shadows of your past and into a brighter tomorrow.

Below, I have listed some next steps you can take. Decide which is right for you and please connect with me if there is something I can do to personally help you on your journey.

Take the FIRST STEPS To Thriving in Recovery again

Each time you go through this program you will gain more from it. These aren't exercises that are intended to be done once in your life. Whether you do them again now or set the workbook aside and revisit in a few months, this workbook will continue to be a valuable tool for your journey. Next time, you may consider completing this workbook with another person, either a sponsor, your friend, or a small group of people you know and trust.

Attend a FIRST STEPS To Thriving in Recovery Workshop

Occasionally, I will present workshops on this material to help people dig deeper into the content and exercises. If you have a group that would be interested in hosting a workshop for your organization or community, please connect with me. My contact information is below.

Join us in the A Life Unchained Facebook Group

It's often said that the opposite of addiction is connection. That's what this group is about. Meet great people, create real connections and find the inspiration, tools, and support to become a happier, more successful, and more fulfilled version of YOU. Visit ALifeUnchained.com to find out more.

Get a FREE Personalized Recovery Assessment and Thriving Strategy Session

Let's take a deeper look at the different areas of your life to see what is working well and where there is an opportunity for some quick improvement. If you would like to schedule a private call with me to learn some ways to create positive changes in your life, send me an email and write "THRIVE" in the subject line. Email me at garret@garretbiss.com

Sick and tired of not being the best version of you? Are you ready to break free from all that's held you back from experiencing your full potential for happiness, fulfillment, success, and inner-peace? I've got three options that may be the best next step for you right now:

Thriving in YOUR Recovery Online [Self-Mastery Course]

This comprehensive online training will guide you through a practical, step-by-step approach to being the best you. This program shares everything you need to know about the science of human flourishing and breaks it down to simple practices you can engage to help you Thrive. Much of the material and exercises shared in this course is evidence-based and have been used to help thousands to experience better lives in recovery. During the course, I will walk you through every step of the way and help you create a personalized plan for getting to where you want to be. Visit ThrivingInYourRecovery.com to find out more and enroll.

Thriving in YOUR Recovery Academy [Group Coaching Program]

All the benefits of the online self-mastery course with the added support of a small group of others on the same journey. Because of the format, this program goes a little deeper and is more customized to the individuals in the group. We go through the same areas of life and similar material but we do it on a schedule that provides pre-dictability, accountability, and support. The group coaching calls give you access to me so you can ensure you have your questions answered and are going through the program in the most effective way. This program also includes some one-on-one coaching sessions to give you personal accountability, as well as multiple group Q&A calls provided to address any questions or issues that are coming up in your recovery. Visit ThrivingInYourRe-covery.com to find out more about the program and apply to be a part of the next group.

Thriving in YOUR Recovery Coaching [Individual Recovery Coaching]

If you would rather work with me one-on-one to receive the greatest level of accountability and personalized support, there are a few options available. If interested, send me an email so we can discuss the options available and if one is a best fit for you: garret@garretbiss.com.

Notes